ECONOMIC EXPERIMENTS

IN THE

CLASSROOM

Denise Hazlett
Whittman Collage

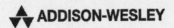 **ADDISON-WESLEY**

An imprint of Addison Wesley Longman, Inc.

Reading, Massachusetts • Menlo Park, California • New York • Harlow, England
Don Mills, Ontario • Sydney • Mexico City • Madrid • Amsterdam

Economic Experiments in the Classroom by Denise Hazlett
Copyright © 1999 Addison Wesley Longman, Inc.

ISBN: 0-321-03366-3

1 2 3 4 5 6 7 8 9 10-VG-02010099

Preface

This supplement to your economics textbook describes nine classroom experiments you can run to illustrate economic theory. The first seven experiments demonstrate the microeconomic concepts of supply and demand, competitive equilibrium, consumer and producer surplus, price ceilings and floors, free trade, excise taxes, monopoly pricing, and diminishing marginal returns. The last two experiments demonstrate the macroeconomic concepts of inflation uncertainty, and exchange rate controls. The experiments can be run in any order, and each can stand alone. However, I do recommend that you first read the introductory chapter which provides general suggestions on how to run experiments, as well as the next chapter, which describes in detail how to run the basic market experiment. Then, you will be set to move on to any of the experiments! Good luck and enjoy experimenting with economics. Your students will.

Contents

Contents

INTRODUCTION

Economic Experiments in the Classroom

Classroom experiments transform students into investigators who demonstrate economic principles for themselves. In the process, students become informed critics of the applications and limitations of economic theory. For instance, a student skeptical of the claim that markets reach equilibrium becomes convinced when he or she observes the effect of the invisible hand in the laboratory. Students will extrapolate from the laboratory to other market situations, coming to recognize the wide-ranging applications of economic principles. What's more, they will consider how the textbook description of a market compares to the many real-world versions. Student thus draw conclusions about how theory fits particular circumstances. While students learn the limits of stylized economic models, they also come to appreciate the ability of the models to predict economic behavior.

Many students learn best by doing. Abstract concepts come alive as students take on experimental roles. The experiment itself provides first-hand experience in a market situation where students may not have any background, such as in the role of a producer. This participation provides an insider's perspective on market behavior students might not otherwise have. In addition, the laboratory experience produces a concrete example that makes tools such as supply and demand easier to understand and to use. Analysis of the experimental results allows students to compare their behavior with theoretical predictions. They draw specific conclusions about the power of economic theory in this special case, and more general conclusions in the abstract.

Conducting Successful Experiments

Running an experiment requires preparation time on the part of the instructor, as well as use of valuable class time. The pay back comes when students become excited participants and enthusiastic analysts of their results. Students remember the conclusions they draw from experiments throughout the semester (and later in their lives!), making the experiments a valuable reference tool during the course. An instructor who is hesitant about the time commitment for preparation and execution can start slowly, doing only one or just a few experiments. Even one market experiment early in the semester can provide the basis for examples that later help introduce complicated concepts.

Each of the experiments in this manual has been thoroughly class-tested. Each takes 30 or fewer minutes to conduct, leaving time for an in-class discussion. Required materials consist of the hand-outs described in this manual, a blackboard, and room for students to maneuver. The experiments work well with almost any size class, from ten students up. Instructors have successfully run versions of these experiments with classes of two hundred, although the experiments do take more time in the larger classes. You can run these experiments in any order you choose. Experiment 1, which describes the basic market framework that most of the other experiments use, makes a logical starting point. You could then move on to whichever experiment fits your goals. You may wish to combine two of the shorter experiments, if your schedule permits. For example, Experiment 1 (the basic supply and demand experiment) combined with Experiment 2 (the shifting demand experiment) makes a 35-minute experiment. If you have 50 minutes to spend experimenting, you could even add Experiment 3 (the price ceiling and price floor experiment), for a total of three experiments in one day.

The experiments in this manual provide frequent opportunities for students to make decisions, so that the activity holds their interest. Students make sufficiently complicated decisions to prevent tedium, but not so complicated as to cause frustration. Each experiment generates data for the students to analyze either in a writing assignment or in class discussion, or both. In order to make the experiment an enjoyable learning exercise and one that generates reliable data, the instructor must ensure that everyone understands the instructions. Otherwise, students will feel frustrated and may take random actions that muddy the results. Reading the instructions aloud as the students follow along on their own copies, with pauses for students to ask questions, keeps students from getting lost. Also, because the instructor knows the equilibrium price and quantity, he or she can watch for out-of-equilibrium trades which indicate a student with problems. Finally, in experiments with fairly complex decisions, student record-keeping sheets help them organize information and remember the experimental set-up.

It generally works best to run an experiment before introducing the theory the experiment demonstrates. If students know how theory suggests they should behave during the course of an experiment, they may believe that this knowledge influenced their results. Students become more firmly convinced of the predictive power of theory if they discover it for themselves. For instance, consider Experiment 3, the price ceiling and price floor experiment. If you run this experiment before giving a lecture on rent control, you will notice that most buyers receive the news of a price ceiling with joy. However, it takes only a few minutes for them to become disillusioned with the idea of a price ceiling helping buyers. The experiment itself makes a great starting point for a lecture on rent control, with the supply and demand curves from the experiment providing the theoretical structure behind the discussion.

Keep in mind one of the guidelines for conducting classroom experiments that carries over from research experiments: never lie to the participants. Do not, for instance, tell them that an experiment will end within three minutes, but then have the experiment continue after this deadline. Once you lose your credibility, students will not believe what you tell them in future experiments. If you raise doubts about the experimental framework, you may make students think they are participating in a different experiment altogether. You would then likely get behavior that looks random and which does not illustrate the point you want to make.

Students need proper motivation to behave as they would in a true market situation, in order to make their experience and results useful. For the experiments described here, the admonition to maximize hypothetical earnings works well. Because they find the exercises interesting, students rise to this challenge. Also, a component of the course grade for on-task participation in the experiments helps ensure that students arrive on time and pay attention. Some instructors like to use extra credit points proportional to the student's experimental earnings, or a small prize for the student with the highest earnings, to provide additional motivation. However, some students will have higher earnings than others simply because they start in more favorable positions. For instance, a seller with a low cost of production has greater potential earnings than a seller with a higher cost. Over the course of several experiments, this random component to earnings will generally average out. An instructor who issues grades (or other goodies) based on experimental earnings might rely on that averaging-out effect. Alternatively, the instructor could calculate each student's earnings as a proportion of the potential earnings for a person in the student's position.

EXPERIMENT 1

The Double Oral Auction

DESCRIPTION OF THE EXPERIMENT

Time required: 20 minutes.

The double oral auction experiment provides a basic introduction to markets, demonstrating how prices determine production and distribution decisions in a competitive economy. Students take the roles of potential buyers and sellers of widgets, a hypothetical good. They begin the experiment knowing only their own cost of production or their own consumption value. As they trade, they begin to see how prices convey information in a decentralized economy. From an initially chaotic set of trades, the market gradually converges to equilibrium.

The instructor issues each buyer a slip with that buyer's ID number and consumption value for one unit of the good. Likewise, the instructor issues each seller a slip with that seller's ID letter and cost of producing one unit of the good. Sellers only incur their cost if they sell their unit. The sellers' costs and buyers' values remain private information. Buyers and sellers mingle in an open area of the room, calling out offers to buy and offers to sell one unit at a price they specify. Either may accept the other's offer. Once an offer gets accepted, both parties come to the front of the room to report the transaction, then they sit on the sidelines waiting for the next period to begin. Each student may trade at most once each period, but has the option of not trading at all. The instructor records information on each transaction (seller's ID letter, buyer's ID number, and the price) on the blackboard for all to see. Seeing these prices helps speed convergence to equilibrium.

The instructor's role thus includes reading the instructions aloud while students follow on their copies, answering questions, and recording data. Otherwise, the instructor lies low and tries not to intervene. In particular, the instructor avoids making suggestions about what prices students should offer or accept. If students feel that the market converged because, for instance, the instructor suggested that buyers pay more and sellers charge less, then they will not credit the power of markets to find the equilibrium price without intervention. The exception to this rule comes in the case of a student who trades at a loss. An instructor who notes such a trade should quietly talk to the student in order to determine which part of the instructions the student does not understand.

Occasionally two traders on the same side of the market, for instance two buyers, mistakenly attempt to trade with each other. The record-keeper will catch this error because the parties report two ID numbers rather than a number and a letter. Both buyers seem quite happy about the low price each has negotiated, until they realize their error. The instructor then sends them back to the trading floor to find sellers. To minimize this type of mistake, a buyer offering to buy at a price of $50 calls out "Buy at $50," whereas a seller shouts, for instance, "Sell at $95." A few mistakes still happen, because of the noise in the room, but the system of number and letter ID's catches these mistakes.

Once all students who wish to trade have done so, the instructor ends that period and starts the next. This second period runs like the first. Students have the same production costs and consumption values as before. However, they now have more information about prevailing prices. This extra information tends to make prices range more tightly around the equilibrium, and quantity move closer to equilibrium as well. Trade continues for a series of market periods, until prices and quantities reach equilibrium. This process takes four or five periods. The length of a period generally depends on the time it takes to record transactions. In a class of 30 students, a period takes three or four minutes. In large classes, an assistant who helps with the recording can keep each period from taking too long. To keep students from wasting time haggling over small price differences, you can restrict students to trading in whole or half prices.

PREPARING FOR THE EXPERIMENT

The instructor prepares a slip for each student before the experiment, listing the student's status as a buyer or seller, his or her experimental ID, and cost or value. Examples of these slips appear in Table 1.1. The instructor arrives early to class to clear the trading floor and start handing out slips. A sign-up sheet like that in Table 1.2 allows the instructor to take attendance and to record which student assumes which role.

Table 1.1. Buyer and Seller Slips

You are Buyer 1.   The value to you of consuming a widget is $32.
You are Seller A.   A widget costs you $21 to produce.

Table 1.2. Student Sign-up Sheet

Buyer's ID	Student's Name		Seller's ID	Student's Name
1			A	
2			B	
3			C	
etc.	etc.		etc.	etc.

The instructor has considerable latitude in devising the production costs and consumption values which underlie the experimental supply and demand. However, the indivisibility of the widgets introduces some complications. For instance, the experimental supply and demand curves will have the step form of Figure 1.1. Because of this complication, it generally works best to design the supply and demand curves to intersect at a specific equilibrium quantity, and over a range of equilibrium prices. Then in equilibrium, everyone who would like to trade at the prevailing prices can find a partner. Figure 1.1 provides an example of supply and demand with a single equilibrium quantity, Q, and a range of equilibrium prices between P and P*. The other ways in which the supply and demand curves could meet have less desirable properties. These alternatives rely on some traders making zero-profit trades. Without these zero-profit trades, someone willing to trade at the prevailing price could not find a partner.

For this first experiment, it would likely work best to have all students able to trade in equilibrium. In general, the existence of sellers with costs above the equilibrium price, and buyers with values below, provides valuable fodder for follow-up discussion. However, in this simple introductory experiment such students quickly become frustrated when they find they cannot trade. In later experiments the instructor can have such students switch values part way through the experiment, so that no one remains unable to trade for long.

Figure 1.1. Sample Supply and Demand Graph.

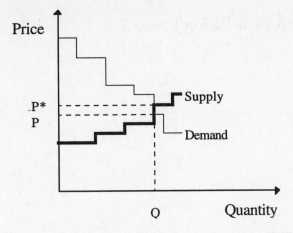

In order to assign students their costs and values, start with a specific price which will fall within the equilibrium price range. Then add one buyer with a value above that price for each seller with a cost below. If you have an odd number of students, the last to arrive could help with record-keeping. Avoid making the supply and demand curves mirror images. Equally steep supply and demand curves would yield equal amounts of consumer and producer surplus. However, students find it more interesting when they discover that the producer and consumer surplus differ. Since students seem to expect gains from trade to be symmetric, deliberately making them asymmetric, as in Figure 1.1, provides food for thought. Similarly, giving the demand and supply curves slightly uneven shapes helps students understand that not all demand and supply curves look the same. Finally, avoid issuing the values and costs in order, with Buyer 1 having the highest value and Seller A the lowest cost, for instance. This ordering of values and costs becomes predictable in future experiments and undoes some of the effect of private information.

Table 1.3 provides an example of buyers' values and sellers' costs for a class of 20. In this example, the equilibrium price ranges from 19 to 21, with an equilibrium quantity of 10. The derivation of supply and demand from this table becomes a more interesting exercise because the buyers' values and sellers' costs do not appear in order. Figure 1.2 provides the supply and demand graph for the data in Table 1.3. Note that producer surplus exceeds consumer surplus in this example.

Table 1.3. Information on Buyers' Values and Sellers' Costs

Buyer's ID	Buyer's Value	Seller's ID	Seller's Cost
1	22	A	11
2	25	B	7
3	23	C	19
4	21	D	14
5	26	E	18
6	22	F	15
7	29	G	5
8	28	H	6
9	26	J	10
10	28	K	11

Figure 1.2. Supply and Demand Graph for the Example Data in Table 2.3.

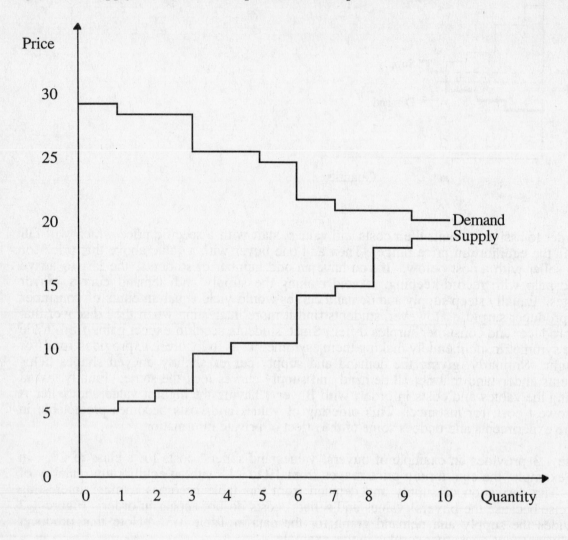

RESULTS

Convergence happens fairly quickly in this experiment. However, students may attempt to collude on prices, which can slow the process. Typically these collusive agreements break down quickly. They merit the time spent on them. Their failure shows the strength of the competitive equilibrium prediction, even in the presence a fairly small number of traders. You could offer to let those who wish to collude step outside in order to (quietly) discuss their plans. This offer helps to give the collusive agreements their best shot. Then, when the collusion breaks down, students get first-hand experience with the power of competitive market forces.

FOLLOW-UP

This experiment can be mined for many economic concepts, from introducing supply and demand to calculating consumer and producer surplus. You may want to let students wrestle with the data from the experiment before the class meets for a discussion. For instance, you could have them derive the theoretical supply and demand curves and find the equilibrium on their own. This individual practice helps cement these concepts. Then as a writing assignment, students could discuss how closely their results corresponded to their theoretical predictions. The questions below could form the basis either for a writing assignment that precedes the discussion, or could serve to start the discussion itself. These question presume that the experiment comes early in the semester, during the introduction of the concepts of supply, demand, and equilibrium. For students to answer these questions, they need the information you recorded on transactions in each period, including the ID's of both parties and the price for each transaction. Be sure to copy this information before erasing the board! Likewise, they need a chart as in Table 1.3, with information on all of the buyers' values and sellers' costs.

QUESTIONS FOR WRITING ASSIGNMENTS AND DISCUSSION

1. Graph the market demand curve for buyers. To graph this demand curve, use the information on buyers' values, not the information on actual trades conducted during the experiment.

2. On the same graph as above, include the market supply curve. To graph the supply curve, use the information on sellers' costs, not the information on actual trades.

3. What does theory predict will be the equilibrium price and quantity traded? To answer this question, use your supply and demand graph, not information on actual trades.

4. Now consider the information on actual trades. Do these experimental results correspond to the equilibrium price and quantity that theory predicts?

5. How do the experimental results change from period to period?

6. How did your earnings in the experiment compare to what theory predicted you would earn in equilibrium?

INSTRUCTIONS FOR THE DOUBLE ORAL AUCTION EXPERIMENT

You are about to participate in an experimental market for a hypothetical good called widgets. Your information slip tells you whether you are a potential buyer and consumer of widgets, or a potential producer and seller of widgets. The experiment will consist of a series of market periods. In each period a buyer may choose to buy one widget, and a seller may choose to sell one widget. No one may trade a fraction of a widget, or more than one widget per period. However, you may opt to trade no widgets at all in a period.

Those of you who are **buyers** have a value on your slip that tells you how much consuming a widget is worth to you. If you buy a widget, you earn the difference between this value and the price that you pay. You should negotiate for the lowest possible price, as long as that price is lower than your value. Never pay a higher price than what a widget is worth to you, or you will make a loss. If you do not buy a widget, you earn zero that period.

Those of you who are **sellers** have a cost of production on your slip. If you sell a widget, you earn the difference between the price and your cost. You should negotiate for the highest possible price, as long as that price is higher than your cost. Never sell a widget for a price lower than your cost of production, or you will make a loss. If you do not sell a widget, you earn zero for that period.

Buyers and sellers make trades using a double oral auction market. Buyers and sellers will mingle and make offers. Buyers call out offers to buy by saying, for example, "Buy at 15," which indicates willingness to buy a unit at a price of 15. Similarly, sellers call out offers to sell by saying, for example, "Sell at 95," which indicates willingness to sell a unit at a price of 95. Any buyer may accept any seller's offer, or vice versa. You may make offers in whole prices or halves. For instance, a buyer or seller may call out a price of 64.5 or 13.0, but not 64.2 or 13.7. When a buyer and seller have agreed on a price, they come to the front of the room and report the price, the buyer's ID number, and the seller's ID letter. I will record this information on the board. The finished buyer and seller then sit at the edge of the trading floor and wait for the next period. When everyone who wishes to has traded, I will end the period and start a new one, in which everyone again has the same costs or values and again may trade at most one unit.

EXPERIMENT 2

A Shift in Demand

DESCRIPTION OF THE EXPERIMENT

Time required: 20 minutes.

This experiment illustrates the effect on price and quantity when demand increases. The instructor begins by announcing that the class will run two experiments: Experiments A and B. Experiment A runs like the basic double oral auction experiment. Students again take the roles of buyers and sellers. After four or five periods, enough for the market to reach equilibrium, the instructor announces that the first experiment has ended and the second experiment will begin. The instructor then issues new information slips to students. Those students who were buyers now become sellers. These new sellers have the same costs as the sellers from the first experiment. Thus both experiments have the same supply curve. The new buyers, however, have different consumption values from the buyers in the first experiment. Buyers have higher consumption values in the second experiment, resulting in an increase in demand. This right-ward shift of the demand curve causes the equilibrium price and quantity to rise.

Students learn from this experiment how a decentralized economy responds to changes in demand. This adjustment process doesn't require anyone to announce that a change has occurred. So, do not volunteer that traders have new values. If students know that demand has increased, they may believe that this knowledge influenced their results. If students ask whether the values or costs in the second experiment differ from those in the first, simply respond with an enigmatic "possibly."

Because students have previous experience with the double oral auction, they will likely trade quickly, allowing you to complete this experiment in 20 minutes. If you can afford to spend a few more minutes on this exercise, you may wish to prepare for a third experiment the same day, in which supply shifts. You would again issue new information slips, this time giving sellers new costs. You could have supply either increase or decrease. The extra experience graphing a shift in supply and finding the new equilibrium may well warrant another ten to twelve minutes spent on the experiment.

PREPARING FOR THE EXPERIMENT

Prepare a sign-up sheet as shown in Table 1.2 and information slips as shown in Table 2.1. Note that each student needs two slips, one for each experiment. Be sure to collect the slips from Experiment A before you hand out the slips for Experiment B, so that students do not confuse their roles. It works well to have traders keep their ID's through both experiments, even as they switch roles. For instance, Buyer 1 in the first experiment becomes Seller 1 in the second. You can then arrange to have the buyers with values below the equilibrium price in the first experiment become sellers with relatively low costs in the second. Thus, a buyer who could not trade in the first experiment becomes a seller who can trade in the second. Likewise, sellers priced out of the market in the first experiment become high-valued buyers in the second. Having these high-cost sellers and low-valued buyers serves a useful pedagogical purpose. For instance, students often believe that society is best served if everyone gets to trade. This experiment provides the background for a discussion on how society can be better off if some people do not trade. However, you would not want to illustrate this point by forcing a student to spend the entire experiment unable to do anything.

Table 2.1. Buyer and Seller Slips for Both Experiments

Experiment A You are Buyer 1.   The value to you of consuming a widget is $39.
Experiment A You are Seller A.   A widget costs you $30 to produce.
Experiment B You are Seller 1. A widget costs you $31 to produce.
Experiment B You are Buyer A. The value to you of consuming a widget is $40.

The experimental results should clearly distinguish between the equilibria in the two experiments. Be sure to choose values for buyers and costs for sellers that result in a higher equilibrium quantity in the second experiment. Also, it works best if the equilibrium price range for the second experiment does not overlap with the price range for the first. Table 2.2 provides sample data for a class of 20. The first experiment has an equilibrium quantity of 7 and price range of 32 to 33. In the second experiment, the quantity rises to 9, with a price range of 34 to 35.

Table 3.2. Buyers' Values and Sellers' Costs for Experiments A and B

Experiment A				Experiment B			
Buyer	Value	Seller	Cost	Buyer	Value	Seller	Cost
1	39	A	30	A	40	1	31
2	31	B	25	B	38	2	25
3	36	C	36	C	49	3	32
4	45	D	32	D	43	4	33
5	42	E	34	E	47	5	34
6	29	F	33	F	46	6	26
7	32	G	31	G	40	7	25
8	34	H	29	H	36	8	29
9	36	J	25	J	35	9	30
10	43	K	26	K	33	10	36

RESULTS

The switching of roles between buyers and sellers may initially mask the change in buyers' values. At first, people will likely try to conduct trades at the old equilibrium price. However, the change in demand will become apparent as buyers bid up the price to get extra units forthcoming. The market converges to the new equilibrium within about four periods.

FOLLOW-UP

Once you give students information on all the sellers' costs, buyers' values, and the trades conducted, they can derive the market supply and demand curves, and find the equilibrium for each experiment. Then, in a writing assignment or in-class discussion (or both), they can describe how well they think economic theory predicted the behavior they observed in the experiment. The following questions work well for individual writing assignments and class discussion.

QUESTIONS FOR WRITING ASSIGNMENTS AND DISCUSSION

1. Graph the supply and demand curve for Experiment A. (Remember to use the information on buyers' values and sellers' costs rather than information on actual trades conducted during the experiments.) What is the equilibrium price and quantity? How closely did the actual trades come to the equilibrium predicted by theory?

2. On the same graph as above, show the supply and demand curve for Experiment B. What is the equilibrium price and quantity, given the supply and demand curve for Experiment B? Consider now the actual trades conducted in Experiment B. Did these trades correspond to the theoretical prediction?

3. What happened to price and quantity traded between Experiment A and Experiment B? Why did this change happen?

4. Are buyers in Experiment A better or worse off than the buyers in Experiment B? Are sellers in Experiment A better or worse off than the sellers in Experiment B?

INSTRUCTIONS FOR EXPERIMENT 2

We will do two experiments today. The experiments will use the double oral auction market that we used before. Those who are buyers in the first experiment today will become sellers in the second. The sellers from the first experiment will likewise become buyers in the second. Your information slip tells you whether you are a buyer or a seller in the first experiment. Let's review the instructions for the double oral auction experiment.

(For a review, see the instructions for Experiment 1, the double oral auction.)

EXPERIMENT 3

Price Ceilings and Price Floors

DESCRIPTION OF THE EXPERIMENT

Time Required: 20 minutes.

This experiment demonstrates the effects of government price controls on quantity, price, and gains from trade. Students again take the roles of buyers and sellers in a double oral auction. After enough periods for the market to reach equilibrium, the instructor announces that the government has imposed a price ceiling at a particular price (below the equilibrium price), so that buyers will not have to pay so much. Buyers react happily to the price ceiling, until they realize that sellers cannot afford to sell as many units at that price. After a few periods with the price ceiling, the instructor announces that the government has imposed a price floor at a particular price (above the equilibrium price), in order to help producers. Producers also react happily until they realize that consumers cannot afford to buy as many units at that price. Before the last period, the instructor announces that the government will not impose any price controls that period.

PREPARING FOR THE EXPERIMENT

Preparation resembles that for the basic double oral auction experiment. You will need a sign-up sheet, as in Table 1.2, and one information slip for each student, as in Table 1.1. In this experiment, it works well to have some buyers with consumption values below the equilibrium price range. These buyers may manage to trade during the price ceiling periods. Their transactions provide interesting discussion material, since these low-valued buyers will displace buyers with higher values. Likewise, sellers with costs above the equilibrium range may get to trade during the price floor periods, but only by displacing lower-cost sellers. Their transactions will provide more fodder for discussion of the effects of government price controls. Thus, when choosing the price ceiling level, choose a price below the consumption values for most (or all) of the buyers. Also, when choosing the price floor level, choose a price above the production cost for most (or all) of the sellers.

RESULTS

In the periods before the price controls, the market quickly converges to equilibrium. It does not take long to run the price ceiling and price floor periods. The trades happen very quickly. Nor do you need many periods to see the shortage develop under a price ceiling or the surplus under a price floor. Two or three periods of each type of control will suffice. In the last period, without any price controls, the market returns to the initial equilibrium.

FOLLOW-UP

This experiment provides a great starting point for a lecture on the minimum wage or rent control. If students first have a chance to analyze the experimental data, they will bring a valuable degree of thoughtful consideration to the discussion. Students will need information on all the sellers' costs, buyers' values, and the trades conducted in order to answer the following questions. With the information you give them, be sure to indicate which periods had price ceilings or floors.

QUESTIONS FOR WRITING ASSIGNMENTS AND DISCUSSION

1. Graph the market supply and demand, and find the theoretical equilibrium, assuming no government intervention.

2. Consider the periods before the government instituted a price ceiling or price floor. Did trade in these periods correspond to the equilibrium predicted by theory?

3. What does theory predict will happen in the periods with the price ceiling? What actually does happen during these periods?

4. Would you say that buyers were happy with the price ceiling which was meant to help them? How would you say a price ceiling affects society as a whole?

5. What does theory predict will happen in the periods with the price floor? What actually does happen?

6. Would you say that sellers were happy with the price floor which was meant to help them? How would you say a price floor affects society as a whole?

INSTRUCTIONS FOR THE PRICE CONTROLS EXPERIMENT

The instructions are the same as for Experiment 1, the basic double oral auction. For experienced students, it should suffice to tell them that they will be conducting a double oral auction experiment. They will remember the experimental set-up from their previous participation.

EXPERIMENT 4

International Trade

DESCRIPTION OF THE EXPERIMENT

Time required: 20 minutes.

The experiment begins with buyers and sellers divided between two double oral auction markets for the same hypothetical good. Each market represents a separate country. For the first few periods, a trade barrier prevents any trade between countries. Each market thus reaches its own individual equilibrium. In Country X, relatively high consumption values and costs result in higher prices for widgets than in Country Y. The instructor records the transactions on the blackboard each period, where everyone can see them. The trades for each country go on separate parts of the board, so that students see the differences between the two markets. After both markets reach equilibrium, the instructor announces that the two countries have negotiated a free trade agreement. Now, buyers and sellers may trade with people from the other country. Equilibrium prices under free trade lie between the prices that prevailed in the separate markets.

The experiment demonstrates that the law of one price holds under free trade, but not under restricted trade. The experiment also shows how a free trade agreement can increase total gains from trade, yet leave some traders worse off. From the perspective of Country X, free trade makes the price fall, leaving its buyers better off and its sellers worse off. From the perspective of Country Y, free trade makes the price rise, leaving its sellers better off and its buyers worse off. So, students gain the individual perspective on free trade of a particular interest group. Then after the experiment ends, students calculate total consumer and producer surplus under restricted trade and under free trade. They see that removing trade barriers makes total gains from trade rise.

PREPARING FOR THE EXPERIMENT

You will need a sign-up sheet as in Table 1.2, and information slips like the examples in Table 4.1. When devising buyers' values and sellers' costs, keep in mind that you do not want to leave anyone unable to trade for the entire experiment. However, some traders will be priced out of the market under free trade, including the highest-cost sellers from Country X and the lowest-valued buyers from Country Y. Since these students cannot trade in the second part of the experiment, you should make sure that they have costs and values that allow them to trade in the first part. Table 4.2 provides example costs and values for a class of 20 in which everyone can trade at some point in the experiment. The highest-cost sellers (Sellers A and C) and the lowest-valued buyers (Buyers 8 and 9) will be the ones priced out of the market under free trade. However, they can trade in the first part of the experiment. The unequal number of buyers and sellers in each country comes from not including traders who would be priced out of the market in both parts of the experiment. For instance, Table 4.2 includes no very-high-cost sellers from Country X because these people would remain unable to trade throughout the entire experiment.

14

Table 4.1. Buyer and Seller Slips

You live in Country X. You are Buyer 1.   The value to you of consuming a widget is $10.
You live in Country X. You are Seller A.   A widget costs you $6 to produce.
You live in Country Y. You are Buyer 7.   The value to you of consuming a widget is $6.
You live in Country Y. You are Seller E.   A widget costs you $2 to produce.

Table 4.2. Buyers' Values and Sellers' Costs For a Class of 20

Country X				Country Y			
Buyer ID	Value	Seller ID	Cost	Buyer ID	Value	Seller ID	Cost
1	10	A	6	7	6	E	2
2	7	B	4	8	4	F	1
3	9	C	6	9	4	G	2
4	11	D	5	10	6	H	3
5	7					J	3
6	8					K	2

In equilibrium for the markets described in Table 4.2, four trades occur each period in each individual market as long as the trade barrier remains in place. Prices range between 7 and 8 in Country X, and between 3 and 4 in country Y. Under free trade, eight units trade at prices between 5 and 6. Note that Buyers 2 and 5 in Country X cannot trade in the first part of the experiment but can in the second. Under restricted trade neither can find a seller in their own country, despite the fact that their consumption values of 7 make them higher-valued buyers than any buyer in the other country! When the trade barrier falls, they find sellers from Country Y. Likewise, Sellers H and J in Country Y cannot trade in the first part of the experiment but can in the second. Under restricted trade, they cannot find buyers in their own country, despite the fact that their costs of 3 make them lower-cost sellers than any of the sellers in the other country! When the trade barrier falls, they find buyers from Country X. Thus, international trade replaces low-valued buyers with high, and high-cost sellers with low. Total gains from trade rise as a result. Consumer and producer surplus under free trade totals 41, versus 29 (17 in Country X and 12 in Country Y) under restricted trade.

RESULTS

The individual markets reach equilibrium within four or five periods. Students will watch the prices recorded for the other market, as well as their own. They will likely anticipate the fall of the trade barrier. Many students can see that they will benefit from the fall, so they eagerly await it. Others see that they will have lower earnings as a result, and so would rather keep the barrier. Once the trade barrier falls, it takes three or four periods for the market to reach equilibrium.

FOLLOW-UP

A quick show of hands following the experiment indicates which traders benefited from free trade and which lost out. The instructor should ask each group to identify themselves, i.e. whether they represent buyers or sellers, and from which country. Students thus immediately see the effect of free trade on particular groups. Once students have the data on buyers' values and sellers' costs, they can calculate the total theoretical consumer and producer surplus under both restricted trade and free trade. Students can then draw conclusions about how theory predicts free trade will affect society as whole, as well as the individual groups within society. Finally, with data on their own transactions, students can compare their experimental results with the theoretical predictions.

QUESTIONS FOR WRITING ASSIGNMENTS AND DISCUSSION

1. Draw the supply and demand curve for Country X. What price and quantity does economic theory predict will trade in Country X, given the restriction on trade with Country Y? How closely did the experimental results come to this prediction?

2. On a separate graph, draw the supply and demand curve for Country Y. What price and quantity does economic theory predict will trade in Country Y, given the restriction on trade with Country X? How closely did the experimental results come to this prediction?

3. Assume the trade barrier is still in place. What total consumer surplus and producer surplus does theory predict for Country X? What total consumer surplus and producer surplus does theory predict for Country Y? How closely did the experimental results come to this prediction?

4. Assume now that the trade barrier falls. On another graph, draw the supply and demand curve for the market composed of all the buyers and sellers from both countries. What price and quantity does economic theory predict will trade now? How closely did the experimental results come to this prediction?

5. What does theory predict for total consumer surplus and total producer surplus, given free trade? How does the surplus generated under free trade compare to the surplus generated under restricted trade? Do you think these countries are better or worse off for having free rather than restricted trade?

INSTRUCTIONS FOR THE INTERNATIONAL TRADE EXPERIMENT

You live in either Country X or Country Y. Each country has a market for the hypothetical good called widgets. You are either a buyer or seller of widgets. Your private information slip tells you which country you live in and whether you are a buyer or seller. A trade barrier exists between Country X and Country Y, so that you may only trade with other people from your own country. Trades will take place using a double oral auction.

(See the instructions from Experiment 1 for a review of the double oral auction.)

EXPERIMENT 5

Posted Offer Market with Taxes

DESCRIPTION OF THE EXPERIMENT

Time required: 25 minutes.

This experiment uses the posted offer market institution to introduce the effects of an excise tax. The posted offer market resembles the markets students know from their day-to-day experience. In the posted offer, each producer offers to sell at a particular price. Buyers take or leave these offers, without negotiation. Laboratory experience with the posted offer shows that the results students observed in the double oral auction experiments carry over to this more typical market setting. Sellers find that they have no freedom to set a price above equilibrium. Sellers therefore display competitive price-taking behavior despite the fact that they explicitly choose their prices, just as many sellers do in the real world. The first part of the experiment thus shows that the posted offer market yields the same equilibrium outcome as the double oral auction. The second part demonstrates the effects of an excise tax. After about five periods, enough for the price and quantity to reach equilibrium, the instructor announces that each seller will have to pay a tax of a certain amount per unit sold. However, the introduction of an excise tax works equally well in a double oral auction, if the instructor prefers that format.

Students will note a difference between this market and the markets they know, namely that sellers incur no production costs for unsold units. One variation on this experiment, if time permits, has sellers incurring production costs for units that do not sell. In this alternative market setting, prices will likely rise to equilibrium from below, because of the risk of setting a price so high that the widget goes unsold.

PREPARING FOR THE EXPERIMENT

You will need a sign-up sheet as in Table 1.2, and buyer and seller information slips as in Table 1.1. When devising values and costs, you may want to have everyone initially able to trade in equilibrium. Then, no one remains unable to trade throughout the entire experiment, even when the excise tax prevents the highest-cost sellers and lowest-valued buyers from trading. Another option for making sure that everyone can trade at some point has buyers and sellers switching roles. During the switch students get new values and costs that allow those priced out of the market earlier to trade. This option has the advantage of allowing each student to experience the roles of buyer and seller. When choosing the tax level, be sure to set the tax high enough to provide distinct equilibrium price ranges before and after the tax.

Sellers write their prices on slips of paper each period, so that each seller selects his price before he knows the others' prices. You will therefore need one small slip of paper for each seller each period. The slips should have a place for the seller to list the number of the period, his or her ID, and price. See Table 5.1 for a copy of the seller's price slip.

Table 5.1. Seller's Price Slip

Period:	Seller's ID:	Price:

Buyers all have an incentive to arrive first to shop, in order to find the cheapest widgets. With everyone equally motivated, luck determines who arrives first. Drawing a buyer's number from a hat, or rolling a die, works well. The next buyer in numerical order then goes second, and so forth. The buying stage goes quickly under this system because the subsequent buyers know when their turns will come. They take the few seconds before their turn (while the instructor records the previous buyer's purchase) to decide which, if any, widget to buy. To save time, you may want to have one of the sellers crossing off the accepted offers on the board while you record the buyers' purchases on paper.

RESULTS

You may find that convergence to equilibrium takes about one period longer in the posted offer market than the double oral auction. Moreover, right after the imposition of the excise tax, sellers often raise their price by the full amount of the tax. It takes two or three more periods for them to find the post-tax equilibrium, with buyers and sellers splitting the economic incidence of the tax.

Since buyers cannot negotiate, they simply search for the cheapest widget left on the board. Buyers may get bored doing only this simple task, so introducing the excise tax provides an interesting addition. However, instead of getting bored, buyers may react to their take-it-or-leave-it role by deciding to collude. They may even explicitly boycott someone they have observed in the past offering a lower price, who they therefore know has a low production cost and could charge less. You should see the seller's face when his or her widget, the cheapest left on the board, gets passed by!

FOLLOW-UP

Writing assignments and class discussion following the experiment can compare the posted offer and double oral auction frameworks and outcomes, and consider the effects of the excise tax on price, quantity and gains from trade.

QUESTIONS FOR WRITING ASSIGNMENTS AND DISCUSSION

1. Compare how closely the double oral auction and the posted offer experimental market set-ups come to the assumptions of a perfectly competitive market.

2. Consider the periods before the tax. Draw the market demand and supply curves. What price and quantity does economic theory predict? What was the pattern of quantity and average prices during these periods? (When calculating average prices, do not include the prices for unaccepted offers.) Did the results correspond to what theory predicts?

3. Consider the periods after the government imposed the per-unit tax. What is the supply curve for sellers now? Does the demand curve change? What price and quantity does economic theory predict now? Does theory predict that the price will rise by the amount of the tax? Did the results correspond to what theory predicts?

4. How much revenue does theory predict the tax will raise? How does theory predict the tax will affect total consumer and producer surplus? What dead-weight loss would the tax cause, according to theory? How did the results compare to these theoretical predictions?

INSTRUCTIONS FOR THE POSTED OFFER EXPERIMENT

You are about to participate in an experiment using a posted offer market. Your information slip tells you whether you are a potential buyer and consumer of widgets (a hypothetical good) or a potential producer and seller of widgets. The experiment will consist of a series of market periods. In each period a seller may sell at most one widget, and a buyer may buy at most one widget. Sellers decide at the beginning of the period what price to charge for a widget. Each seller privately writes on a slip of paper the price he or she is charging for a widget, without letting other sellers see this price. Once all the sellers have filled out their slips, I will collect these slips and list on the board the prices of all the widgets offered for sale that period. Each buyer will have a turn to announce which widget (if any) he or she wishes to buy. Buyers may not negotiate on the price. If the list does not include a widget at a price the buyer can afford, then he or she passes. The period ends when all buyers have had a turn to buy a widget.

Those of you who are **sellers** have a cost of production on your slip. Never set a price below your cost, or you will make a loss. If a buyer purchases the widget you are offering, you earn the difference between your price and your cost. If no buyer purchases your widget, then you earn zero for that period. You do not incur your production cost unless someone actually buys your widget.

Once all the sellers' prices are listed on the board, each of you who are **buyers** will have a turn to buy a widget. Your information slip tells you how much a widget is worth to you. If the cheapest widget left on your turn has a price lower than your value, then you should buy it. Otherwise you should pass. Never pay more than your value, or you will make a loss. Buyers all have an incentive to arrive first to shop, in order to find the cheapest widgets. With everyone equally motivated, luck determines who actually arrives first. I will pull a number from a hat to determine which buyer goes first. If I draw the number 7, for instance, then Buyer 7 goes first, and Buyer 8 next, with all the other buyers following in numerical order.

EXPERIMENT 6

Monopoly

DESCRIPTION OF THE EXPERIMENT

Time required: 30 minutes.

This experiment demonstrates what happens when a competitive industry becomes monopolized. Students take the roles of sellers in a posted offer market. The instructor determines the market demand schedule in advance, but does not issue the buyers' values to students. Instead, the instructor simulates the buyers. The market starts out competitive, with producers operating independently. Each may sell at most one unit. They incur their production costs only if they sell a unit. Every period, each producer privately writes his price on a slip of paper, then hands the slip to the instructor. The instructor arranges these offers in increasing order of price, then compares them with the market demand schedule which lists buyers' values in declining order. The instructor matches offers with buyers, as long as buyers' values are at least as high as the asking price. The instructor announces aloud all accepted price offers, for the sellers' information, plus the lowest price that did not sell. After enough periods for the market to reach equilibrium, the instructor announces that the sellers have just merged their individual factories into one firm. Each of the factories can still produce one unit at the same cost as before. However, sellers now operate together, choosing one price and a quantity they will jointly offer at that price. As the monopoly restricts its output in order to raise its price, some of the factories that produced before will no longer do so, but their former owners will share in the monopolist's profits. You may wish to designate a chief executive officer from among the students in order to speed the decision-making process.

If you have 45 minutes to spend on the experiment, you may want to have half the class take the roles of buyers, making the set-up more realistic. Real buyers may attempt to revolt against the rising prices. These attempts to collude will likely break down quickly, but their very failure emphasizes the market power a monopoly possesses. Another variation, if time permits, has the sellers merge into a duopoly before they become a monopoly. This variation provides for a subsequent discussion of oligopolies.

PREPARING FOR THE EXPERIMENT

You will need a sign-up sheet listing the ID's of sellers only. Each student needs a seller's information slip with an ID and a cost of production. When devising the market demand schedule, having it step-wise linear as in Table 6.1 makes determining marginal revenue easier, which helps the monopoly find its profit-maximizing price and quantity faster. For the early periods in which sellers operate independently, you will need one price slip, as in Table 5.1, per seller per period. After the sellers merge, they do not need price slips, as they simply announce aloud the price and quantity they have agreed on. Students can calculate their monopoly profits faster if you provide them with a table that lists each factory's cost of production in increasing order, and that gives the total cost at each level of output. For example, suppose you initially have twenty sellers with the costs given in Table 6.2. Once these firms merge, you would issue students Table 6.3, which describes the monopoly's marginal and total costs. Note that having Table 6.3 prepared in advance means that if one of the students does not show up to class, the table no longer applies. To

20

leave some latitude in the event of absences, you could plan to have a few sellers partnered in the first part of the experiment. For instance, the data below for 20 sellers could apply for a class of 24, in which the instructor expects at most four absences. Then, if everyone does come, pairs of students would run four of the individual firms for the competitive part of the experiment.

Table 6.1. The Market Demand Schedule

Quantity	Buyer's Value	Quantity	Buyer's Value
1	33	11	23
2	32	12	22
3	31	13	21
4	30	14	20
5	29	15	19
6	28	16	18
7	27	17	17
8	26	18	16
9	25	19	15
10	24	20	14

Table 6.2. Individual Seller's Costs

Seller ID	Cost of Production	Seller ID	Cost of Production
A	5	K	5
B	4	L	6
C	5	M	7
D	7	N	8
E	9	O	10
F	10	P	12
G	11	Q	4
H	11	R	8
I	12	S	10
J	3	T	13

Table 6.3. The Monopoly's Costs

Quantity	Marginal Cost	Factory Where Unit is Produced	Total Cost	Quantity	Marginal Cost	Factory Where Unit is Produced	Total Cost
1	3	J	3	11	8	R	62
2	4	Q	7	12	9	E	71
3	4	B	11	13	10	F	81
4	5	A	16	14	10	O	91
5	5	K	21	15	10	S	101
6	5	C	26	16	11	G	112
7	6	L	32	17	11	H	123
8	7	D	39	18	12	P	135
9	7	M	46	19	12	I	147
10	8	N	54	20	13	T	160

RESULTS

In the above example, the perfectly competitive equilibrium has a quantity of 20 and a price of 14, whereas the monopoly maximizes profit with a quantity of 12 and a price of 22. Once merged into one firm, the students will try increasing the price above the competitive level and find that they like the resulting increase in profits. If you run this experiment before introducing the theory of the monopoly, the price increases will likely be rather small and tentative until the students start seeing a pattern. However, letting students discover contrived scarcity on their own warrants the extra time spent while the students search out the demand curve. Thirty minutes should suffice for students to find the profit-maximizing price, because the monopoly periods with the instructor simulating the buyers move fast.

FOLLOW-UP

It works best to run this experiment just before introducing the theory of the monopoly in lecture. The following questions then ask students to apply the theory to an analysis of their experimental results.

QUESTIONS FOR WRITING ASSIGNMENTS AND DISCUSSION

1. Consider the periods in which sellers each operated independently. Draw the industry supply and demand curves. What is the price and quantity predicted by economic theory? What are the potential gains from trade (i.e. the sum of consumer and producer surplus in equilibrium)? How close did the actual trades come to achieving the theoretical price and quantity? How close did the actual consumer surplus and producer surplus come to the amount predicted by economic theory?

2. Consider the periods after the firms merged into a monopoly. Draw the monopolist's marginal cost curve. (Do **not** call this curve the market supply curve. A monopolist does not have a supply curve.) Draw the demand curve, and the monopolist's marginal revenue curve. What quantity does economic theory predict a profit-maximizing monopolist would produce? What price would the monopolist charge? What would be the monopolist's profit? What would be consumer surplus? How close did the actual price and quantity traded come to these theoretical predictions? What do you think accounts for the pattern of price and quantity traded over these periods? Calculate the consumer surplus for the period in which the monopolist earned the most profits. How does this consumer surplus compare to the consumer surplus under perfect competition?

INSTRUCTIONS FOR THE MONOPOLY EXPERIMENT

For the first part of the experiment, when sellers operate independently, the instructions are the same as those for Experiment 5. The instructions for the second part are given below.

The sellers have just merged their individual factories into one firm, which is the sole producer of widgets, and is therefore a monopoly. Students must agree on a single price for the monopoly's product, and a quantity to offer at that price. Each of the factories can still produce at most one unit at the same cost as it could before the merger. I will now hand out a table which combines the information on the costs of each factory, in order to list the monopolist's costs of operation at each quantity of output.

EXPERIMENT 7

Diminishing Marginal Returns

DESCRIPTION OF THE EXPERIMENT

Time required: 20 minutes.

In this experiment, students produce peanut butter and jelly sandwiches.[1] Students gradually add their labor to a fixed capital stock comprised of one table, three loaves of sandwich bread, three butter knives, three plates, a jar of jelly, a jar of peanut butter, and a box of sandwich bags. The production process requires spreading jelly on one slice of bread, peanut butter on another, putting the slices together with the spreads on the inside, slicing the sandwich diagonally, and inserting both halves into a sandwich bag. The bread may touch the plates but not the table. Students may store the bagged sandwiches on the table, but a sandwich that falls to the floor does not count. Initially, one student volunteer makes as many sandwiches as he or she can in 30 seconds. Then, another volunteer joins the first and they work together for 30 seconds. A third volunteer then joins the first two for another 30 seconds, and so forth. The class records the marginal product of labor as each worker joins the production team. As the workers specialize, they initially achieve increasing marginal returns. Eventually they exhaust their opportunities for specialization and instead experience congestion, so that diminishing marginal returns set in. Depending on your time constraint, you may wish to continue the experiment until the marginal product becomes negative.

PREPARING FOR THE EXPERIMENT

If you can, bring a stop-watch or a watch with a second hand to class. If you do not have one, a student likely will and you can ask that person to time the workers. In any case, it works well to have a student do the timing. If you have the workers wear plastic food preparation gloves, then you can hand out the sandwiches afterwards for the class to eat. You may even want to bring a beverage, since peanut butter can make people pretty thirsty!

RESULTS

Class output will not necessarily grow in the smooth manner graphed in the textbook. Students may try out various assembly line processes during the course of the experiment. Hitting on a particularly successful rearrangement could even make the marginal product of labor rise again after a period of falling. Nonetheless, students will gain a firm grasp of why production initially exhibits increasing marginal returns. They will either have been one of the team members figuring out how to make the best use of opportunities for specialization, or one of the other class members making suggestions from the audience. Typically, about the same time diminishing marginal returns set in, the student workers will start pointing out which part of the capital stock serves as the limiting factor, as in "if only we had a larger table, so we didn't keep bumping into each other!" So, even if the results

---

[1] The author would like to thank Cynthia Hill for suggesting peanut butter and jelly sandwiches as the product in this experiment.

23

do include anomalies like diminishing marginal returns setting in more than once, the experience does drive home the limits of specialization given a fixed capital stock.

FOLLOW-UP

During the experiment, the instructor updates a table of total product and marginal product of labor, as in Table 6.1. Students refer to this table during the follow-up discussion.

Table 6.1. Marginal Product of Labor

Quantity of Labor	Total Product	Marginal Product of Labor
1		
2		
3		
4		
5		
6		

QUESTIONS FOR WRITING ASSIGNMENTS AND DISCUSSION

1. At what point did diminishing marginal returns set in?

2. What caused the initial increasing marginal returns?

3. What caused diminishing marginal returns to set in?

4. Is every production process subject to the law of diminishing marginal returns?

INSTRUCTIONS

For this experiment, the instructor need not hand out a set of instructions. It suffices to explain that students will produce peanut butter and jelly sandwiches, and to describe the production process. The instructor then asks for a volunteer to do the timing and a volunteer to start producing.

EXPERIMENT 8

Inflation Uncertainty

DESCRIPTION OF THE EXPERIMENT[2]

Time required: 30 minutes.

Students take the roles of lenders and borrowers in a double oral auction. Borrowers have the opportunity to undertake investment projects with relatively high real returns. However, they have no funds of their own with which to finance their projects. Lenders do have funds. Lenders also have the opportunity to undertake investment projects, but their projects have relatively low real returns. Gains from trade reach their maximum when all of the lenders arrange to loan their funds to the borrowers. Thus, the highest-valued projects get financed. However, borrowers and lenders contract for loans in nominal terms, which makes the loans risky. Their payoffs depend on the real returns on the loans, which in turn depend on the inflation rate. Students find out the inflation rate after they have negotiated their loan contracts. The instructor rolls a die to determine the inflation rate. Inflation uncertainty makes loans risky because unexpectedly high inflation benefits borrowers, but harms lenders by an equal amount. Unexpectedly low inflation has the opposite effects. The experiment demonstrates these welfare effects. It also shows that if participants exhibit risk aversion, then inflation uncertainty prevents the credit market from operating effectively. That is, some risk averse borrowers and lenders cannot agree on a nominal interest rate that provides enough of a risk premium for each party. They therefore do not arrange a loan. So, instead of lending their funds to those with higher-valued projects, the potential lenders finance their own lower-valued projects.

The instructor first runs a few periods with zero inflation to establish the equilibrium real interest rate in the absence of inflation. At the beginning of the next period, the instructor announces that the inflation rate will be 4% with certainty. The instructor will likely need to run only one period with perfectly anticipated inflation, since most borrowers and lenders will simply adjust their nominal interest rate bids and offers up by 4%. In later periods, the instructor introduces inflation uncertainty by announcing at the beginning of each period that the inflation rate will be 3%, 4% or 5% with equal probability, determined by the roll of a die. If time permits, the instructor can also run a few periods where a roll of the die determines whether the inflation rate will be 2%, 3%, 4%, 5% or 6%.

PREPARING FOR THE EXPERIMENT

You will need information slips for participants, as in Tables 8.1 and 8.2. The slips list each person's letter ID, the real interest rate on that person's project, and whether the person starts each period with funds of $100 or $0. Those who start with $100 can lend their funds or use them for their own project, whereas those who start with $0 can only finance their project by borrowing. Table 8.3 provides sample buyers' and lenders' values for a class of 20. Note that people A through L start each period with $100, and have relatively low valued projects compared to people M through W, who start each period with

---

[2] The author gratefully acknowledges Jeffrey Parker's help designing the inflation uncertainty experiment.

no funds. Thus, people A through L constitute the potential lenders in the experiment, and M through W the potential borrowers.

Table 8.1. A Sample Lender's Information Slip

Your ID letter is A.
Your project provides a real interest rate of 2.0%.
You start each period with $100.

Table 8.2. A Sample Borrower's Information Slip

Your ID letter is R.
Your project provides a real interest rate of 4.0%.
You start each period with no funds.

Table 8.3. Values for a Class of 20

ID	Funds	Real interest rate on project
A	$100	2.0
B	$100	3.0
C	$100	2.5
D	$100	1.0
E	$100	2.0
F	$100	1.5
H	$100	3.0
J	$100	2.5
K	$100	1.5
L	$100	2.5
M	no funds	4.5
N	no funds	5.5
O	no funds	4.5
P	no funds	6.0
R	no funds	4.0
S	no funds	5.0
T	no funds	4.0
U	no funds	5.0
V	no funds	5.5
W	no funds	4.5

Occasionally students will misread their information slips and conclude, for instance, that they start each period with $100, when in fact they start with $0. To catch such mistakes before the experiment begins, have students initially take positions on different sides of the room, depending on whether they start with $100 or $0. Then you can make sure that you have an equal number of potential lenders and borrowers.

A student record-keeping sheet as in Table 8.4 makes the process of calculating profits clearer, and helps students keep track of how well they are doing. Note that profits do not carry over from one period to the next. Each period is completely separate from the last.

Table 8.4. Student Record-Keeping Sheet

Period	ID of Lender	ID of Borrower	Nominal interest rate on your loan i	Inflation rate π	Real interest rate on your loan $r = i - \pi$	If you lent: profits are real interest rate on loan	If you borrowed: profits are real interest rate on project minus the real interest rate on loan	If you did not borrow and have no funds: profits are 0	If you invested your own $100 in your project: profits are real interest rate on project
1									
2									
3									
4									
5									
6									
7									
8									
9									
10									
11									
12									
13									
14									
15									
16									
17									
18									
19									
20									

RESULTS

Consider the sample values in Table 8.3. In the periods with zero inflation, the equilibrium nominal interest rates range between 3% and 4%, with a quantity of 10 loans. With perfectly anticipated inflation of 4%, the equilibrium nominal rates range between 7% and 8%, again with 10 loans. Once the instructor introduces inflation uncertainty, risk averse lenders will want higher rates, and risk averse borrowers will want lower rates, as compensation for the risk. Those traders with a high degree of risk aversion, or the traders with the least to gain from a loan (the borrower with the 4% real return on the project and the lender with the 3% real return on the project) may not find a mutually acceptable nominal interest rate. The lenders would then opt to undertake their own lower-valued projects, making overall gains from trade fall. On the other hand, undertaking the loan provides for positive expected profits which may overcome the disadvantage of the risk. Moreover, some students like to gamble, and so will enjoy having their profit depend on the roll of a die. Finally, because the experiment has students gambling with hypothetical profits, they may exhibit more risk-loving behavior than they would with their own money at stake. So, whether inflation uncertainty reduces overall gains from trade depends on the participants and their attitudes toward risk. The author has run this experiment several times and always found that inflation uncertainty did reduce overall gains from trade, but the extent varied from class to class.

FOLLOW-UP

It works best to run this experiment after introducing the Fisher equation relationship between nominal interest rates, real interest rates and inflation. The experiment reinforces this relationship, as well as demonstrating the effects of inflation uncertainty on borrowers' and lenders' profits. If you run the experiment before a class discussion on the costs of inflation, then the experiment serves to introduce the difference between anticipated and unanticipated inflation. Note that to answer the questions below, students will need the data from Table 8.3 and information on the inflation rate each period.

QUESTIONS FOR WRITING ASSIGNMENTS AND DISCUSSION

1. Consider the periods when everyone knew there would be no inflation. Given the real interest rates on participants' projects, what does economic theory predict will be the nominal interest rate and quantity of loans? Explain, with reference to the theoretical supply and demand curves for funds. How closely did the experimental results match the behavior predicted by economic theory?

2. What does theory predict will be the nominal interest rate and quantity of loans in the period when everyone knows there will be an inflation rate of 4%? Explain how you found your answer. How close are the actual results to the theoretical predictions?

3. How did participants deal with inflation uncertainty? Did the nominal interest rates and quantity of loans change when inflation uncertainty was added, and as inflation uncertainty increased? How would you describe participants' attitudes toward the risk associated with inflation uncertainty? How did inflation uncertainty affect investment in the projects?

INSTRUCTIONS FOR THE INFLATION UNCERTAINTY EXPERIMENT

1. You are about to participate in an experiment involving a market for loans. The experiment will consist of a series of market periods. Each period you have the opportunity to invest in a productive project that earns the **real** interest rate shown on your information slip. Your project's real interest rate is the amount by which your purchasing power would increase if you invested in your project. Different people have projects that yield different real rates. Each project requires an investment of $100 and may only be undertaken once each period. Each project is over at the end of the period.

2. Your information slip tells you how much money you start each period with. Some of you start each period with $100. Those of you who have $100 have two options each period: (1) you may invest your $100 in your own project, or (2) you may lend your $100 to someone else who will invest it in his project. The rest of you start each period with no funds, though you can finance your project by borrowing $100 from someone else. Regardless of what you do in a particular period, you will start the subsequent period with the funds (either $100 or zero) specified on your information slip, and nothing else. That is, each market period is completely separate from the others.

3. You may borrow or lend only once in each period, but you may also choose not to borrow or lend. Borrowers and lenders will contract for loans in terms of a **nominal** interest rate. The nominal interest rate specifies how many dollars will be repaid as a percentage of the $100 borrowed. The market institution is the double-oral auction. All transactions must be for exactly $100 and all must be expressed in tenths of a percentage point. So, it's okay to offer 10.3%, or 2.4%, but not 10.37% or 2.444%.

4. Once you have agreed upon a transaction, come to the front of the room and report it to me, and I will post it on the board. Once everyone who wishes to has entered into a contract, the loan market closes. After the loan market closes, you will find out what the inflation rate has been over that period. For the first few periods, there will be no inflation. In subsequent periods, I will roll a die to determine the inflation rate for that period. At the beginning of every period, I will announce whether there will be inflation that period and, if so, how the die roll will determine the inflation rate.

5. Your goal is to maximize your profits. Consider first those of you who start with $100 each period. If you lend, then your profits are the real interest rate you earned on the loan. You should lend only if you would earn a higher real interest rate from the loan than your project provides. Otherwise, you should invest in your own project, thereby earning profits equal to the real interest rate on your project. Consider now those of you who start each period with no funds. If you borrow, then your profits are the real interest rate you earned on your project minus the real interest rate you paid for your loan. You should borrow only if your project provides a higher real interest rate than you would pay on your loan. Otherwise, you should do nothing, thereby earning profits of zero. Since you must contract in nominal terms, you will have to subtract the inflation rate from the nominal interest rate in order to calculate the real interest rate on your loan.

6. Please keep track of your actions on your record-keeping sheet. For each period, record your own ID letter in the borrower or lender column, depending on your actions that period. In the other column, record the ID of the person with whom you contracted. Record the nominal interest rate of your loan, the inflation rate, and the real interest rate on your loan. If you did not borrow or lend, leave all these spaces blank. Next, calculate and record your profits for that period. Note that you will record your profits in *one* of the last four columns, depending on what you did that period. Do not try to fill in more than one of the last four columns each period.

EXPERIMENT 9

Exchange Rate Controls in a Developing Country

DESCRIPTION OF THE EXPERIMENT

Time required: 30 minutes.

Students take the roles of traders in a developing country. These traders either desire to acquire foreign currency (dollars) so that they can import goods from the U.S., or they have foreign currency because of exports to the U.S. Their government has an official overvalued exchange rate at which it trades some currency. The government established the overvalued exchange rate in order to avoid the inflationary effects of a depreciation. However, the government does not have enough foreign currency reserves to meet demand at the official rate. So, an unofficial parallel market handles the excess demand. After the government conducts its trades, the parallel market opens, using a double oral auction. Importers would all like to purchase foreign currency cheaply at the official rate. However, exporters would rather trade on the parallel market where they can get a higher price for their foreign currency. The government must thus coerce exporters into trading at the official rate. Moreover, the government must decide who among all the importers will have the privilege of buying this foreign currency. So, the instructor draws ID's from a hat to determine which importers get to buy at the official rate and which exporters must sell. Coercing exporters into selling costs the government resources, because it requires auditing the exporters' books. The government therefore only forces twenty percent of the exporters to trade at the official rate. Thus the government can only sell foreign currency to twenty percent of the importers.

The experiment demonstrates that an overvalued official rate benefits importers but hurts exporters. In fact, some exporters even exit the industry in fear of being forced to trade their foreign currency at the official rate. Thus, the overvalued rate suppresses international trade. Furthermore, the government must decide which exporters to coerce, and which importers to reward. Students see the potential for graft from the government making these decisions. Finally, the experiment shows that the parallel market exchange rate approximates the free market value of the currency, provided the government does not penalize trade in the parallel market.

PREPARING FOR THE EXPERIMENT

You will need to prepare to draw importers' numbers from a hat, and exporters' letters from another hat, to determine who trades with the government. You will also need information slips as in Table 9.1. An exporter's slip lists his or her cost of production in the domestic currency (called the whittie). Every exporter can sell his or her good for $100 in the U.S. Every importer pays $100 to import his or her good from the U.S. An importer's information slip lists the price, in whitties, at which the importer can sell his or her good domestically. Thus, importers wish to buy $100, whereas those who exported have $100 to sell in the foreign exchange market. Table 9.2 provides sample exporter costs and importer prices for a class of 20. For this example, the government sets the official exchange rate at 2 whitties to the dollar.

Table 9.1. Information Slips for an Importer and an Exporter

You are Importer 1.	You are Exporter A.
You can sell your good for 300 whitties.	The cost of producing your good is 185 whitties.

Table 9.2. Exporters' Costs and Importers' Prices

Exporter ID	Exporter's cost of production in whitties	Importer ID	Price in whitties at which importer can sell his good
A	185	1	300
B	190	2	295
C	195	3	290
D	200	4	285
E	205	5	280
F	210	6	275
G	215	7	270
H	220	8	260
J	225	9	250
K	230	10	240

RESULTS

Consider the data from Table 9.2. In a free market, the equilibrium exchange rate would be 2.3 to 2.4 whitties to the dollar. The parallel market clears at about this range also, depending on who participates. Thus, all the importers prefer the official rate of 2.0 whitties to the dollar, and all the exporters prefer the parallel market rate. Each period the government randomly chooses two exporters and two importers to trade at the official rate. Exporters E through K would incur losses if forced to trade at the official rate, so some of them may choose not to export at all. Note that the rate in the parallel market depends on whether marginal traders such as Exporter K and Importer 10 participate. For instance, if Exporters J and K both opt not to export, and Importer 10 happens to get chosen to buy dollars from the government, then the parallel market equilibrium exchange rate range becomes 2.2 to 2.5 whitties to the dollar. So, the range of exchange rates in the parallel market may be wider than in a market without government intervention.

QUESTIONS FOR WRITING ASSIGNMENTS AND DISCUSSION

1. Graph the supply and demand for dollars, assuming that the government plays no role in the foreign exchange market. On your graph, put the quantity of dollars (in hundreds of dollars) on the horizontal axis, and the exchange rate (the number of whitties it takes to buy a dollar) on the vertical axis. What exchange rate does theory predict for the unrestricted market? How many dollars would trade in equilibrium in this market?

2. Explain whether the official rate of 2 whitties per dollar corresponds to the theoretical free-market value of the whittie which you found in Question 1. Did the experimental exchange rates in the parallel market correspond to the theoretical free market value?

3. Did importers wish to trade at the official rate? Did exporters? Would you say that forcing exporters to trade at the official rate is good for international trade? What might actual importers or exporters do to influence the government's decision about who trades at the official rate?

INSTRUCTIONS FOR THE EXCHANGE RATE EXPERIMENT

1. You are about to participate in an experiment in foreign exchange trade, which will last for several periods. You are all citizens of Whit, which is a developing country. Your country's currency is called the whittie. Each of you represents a firm that engages in trade with the United States. Half of you export a good to the U.S., and the other half import a good from the U.S. Your private information slip tells you whether you are an exporter or an importer. I represent the government of Whit, which has established an official exchange rate of 2 whitties for one dollar.

2. **Exporters.** Exporters may sell one good to the U.S. each period, at a price of $100. However, an exporter may choose to sell no goods in a period. An exporter who sells a good to the U.S. will then trade his $100 proceeds on the foreign exchange market for whitties. Each exporter has a cost of producing his good, in whitties, which is given on his private information slip. Exporters may each have a different cost of production, since each produces a different good. An exporter's profits in a period are the amount of whitties he gets in exchange for his $100, minus his cost of production. An exporter therefore wishes to trade his $100 for the greatest amount of whitties he can get. The more whitties he receives, the higher his profits will be.

3. **Importers.** Importers may buy one good from the U.S. each period, for a price of $100. In order to buy a good, importers must first acquire $100 on the foreign exchange market. Each importer has a price, in whitties, at which he can sell the good he imports. This price is given on the importer's private information slip. Importers may each have a different price at which they can sell their good, since each imports a different good. An importer's profits in a period are the difference between the price in whitties he gets for his imported good, and the amount of whitties he pays on the foreign exchange market for the $100 required to import his good. An importer therefore wishes to pay as few whitties as possible for the $100 he acquires on the foreign exchange market. The fewer whitties he pays, the higher his profits will be.

4. At the beginning of each period, exporters decide whether they will sell a good to the U.S. An exporter who does not sell a good to the U.S. will have no activities that period. An exporter who sells a good to the US has $100 which he will sell in the foreign exchange market. Once all the exporters have decided whether or not to sell a good, the official foreign exchange market opens, and transactions with the government occur at the rate of 2 whitties per dollar. A random government audit of firms will determine which firms transact with the government at the official rate. After trade in the official market ends, those who have not just traded with the government may now trade with each other in a parallel market for dollars. There are no government penalties for trading on the parallel market. The parallel market will take the form of a double oral auction, in which importers call out offers to buy $100 dollars at a price they specify, and exporters call out offers to sell $100 at a price they specify. All foreign exchange transactions must be for $100. An importer cannot buy more than $100, but he may choose to buy $0. Once an offer has been accepted, the transaction is complete, and both parties will come to the front of the room to report the price of the trade and the identities of both parties. Once everyone who wishes to has traded, then the parallel market closes. The importers who acquired $100 then buy a good from the U.S., and the period ends. A new period then begins, in which exporters again decide whether to sell a good to the U.S.

NOTES

NOTES

NOTES

NOTES

NOTES

NOTES

NOTES

NOTES

NOTES

NOTES